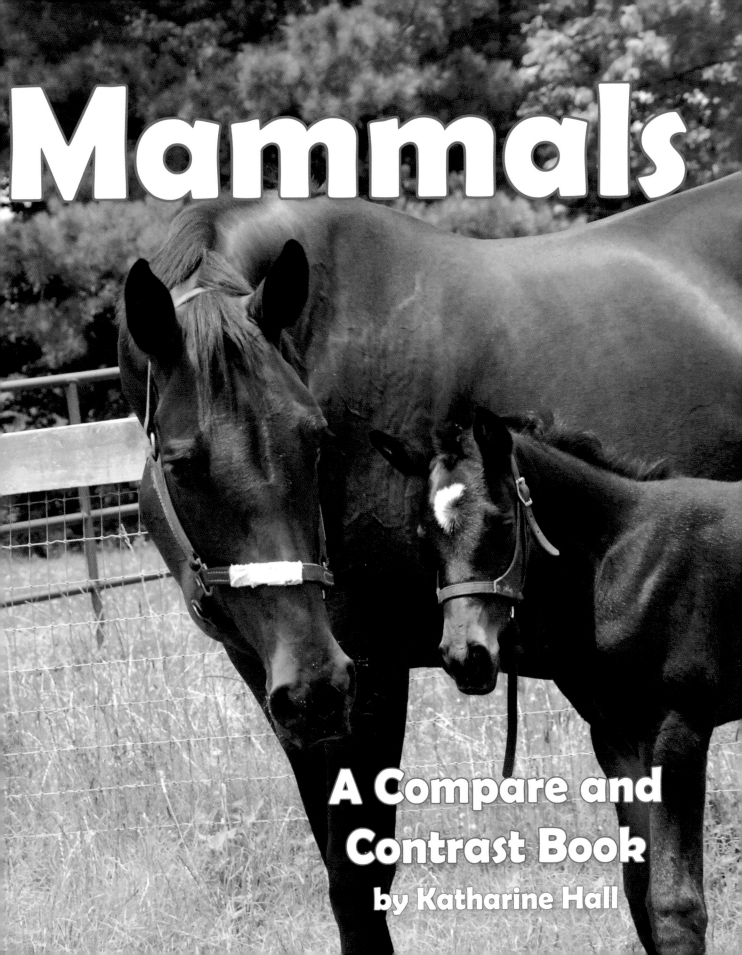

Mammals

A Compare and Contrast Book

by Katharine Hall

There are many kinds of mammals that live in diverse habitats all around the world. Some mammals live on land. Other mammals live in rivers and oceans.

All mammals, even ones that live in water, have lungs and breathe oxygen from the air.

This silverback gorilla breathes
air through his nose.

This Indo-Pacific humpback
dolphin breathes air through
a blowhole on top of her head.

Mammals are a type of vertebrate animal. All mammals have a spine or spinal column.

A mammal's skeleton supports its body.
This cat skeleton has a spine that connects
the head bones (skull) all the way to the tail.

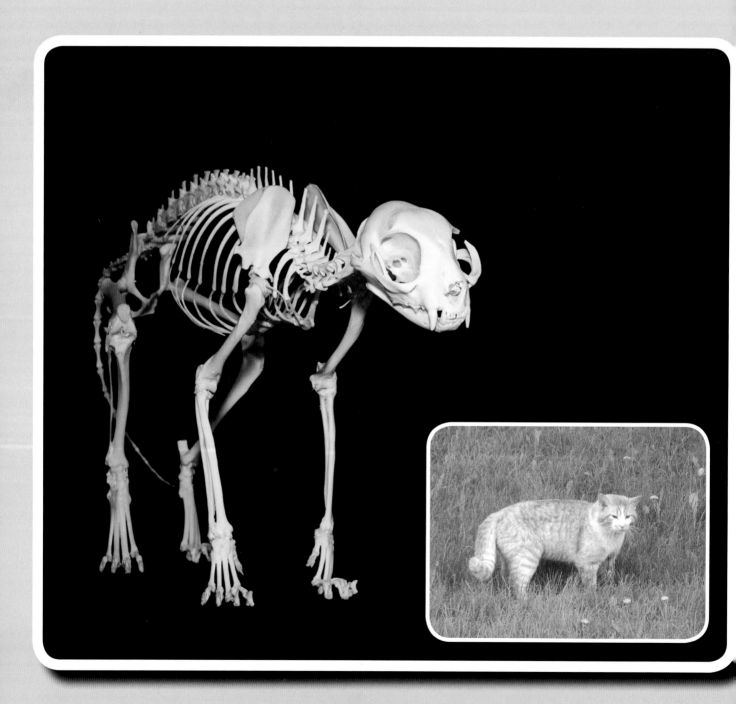

This dolphin skeleton has a spine that connects the skull all the way to the tail.

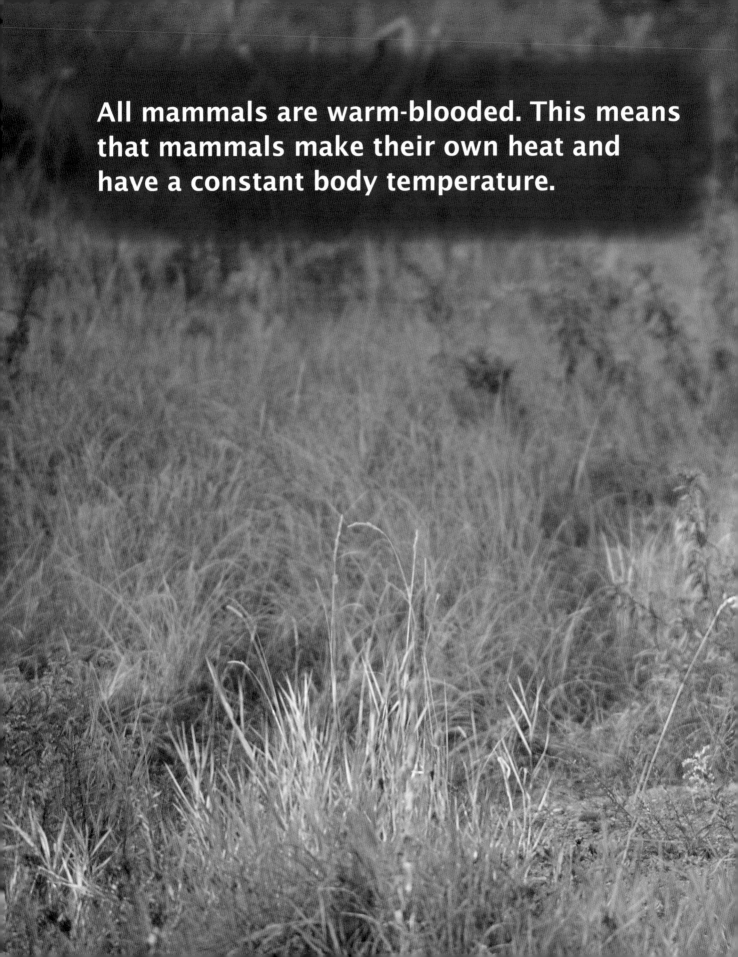

All mammals are warm-blooded. This means that mammals make their own heat and have a constant body temperature.

If goats get too hot, they can sweat or pant to help cool down.

Sea otters have thick fur to keep icy water away from their bodies. This helps them stay warm even when it is cold.

All mammals have hair or fur on their bodies.

This grizzly bear has thick,
soft hair all over her body.

This manatee has sparse
hair all over his body.

Most mammals give birth to live young.

A newborn horse is called a foal. Foals can stand up and walk within two hours of birth.

Newborn sea lions are called pups. Pups can stand only thirty minutes after birth. They get their first swimming lessons when they are a few weeks old.

All mammals feed milk to their young.

A newborn baboon is called an infant. These infants sit in their mother's lap to drink milk.

A newborn whale is called a calf. This beluga whale calf swims beside her mother to drink milk.

There are many different types of mammals living all around the world. You are a mammal too!

For Creative Minds

Dichotomous Key

A dichotomous key helps to sort (classify) animals. These keys work by asking yes or no questions. Each answer leads to another yes or no question, until the animal class is identified. Use the dichotomous key below to learn what defines mammals, birds, reptiles, amphibians, and fish.

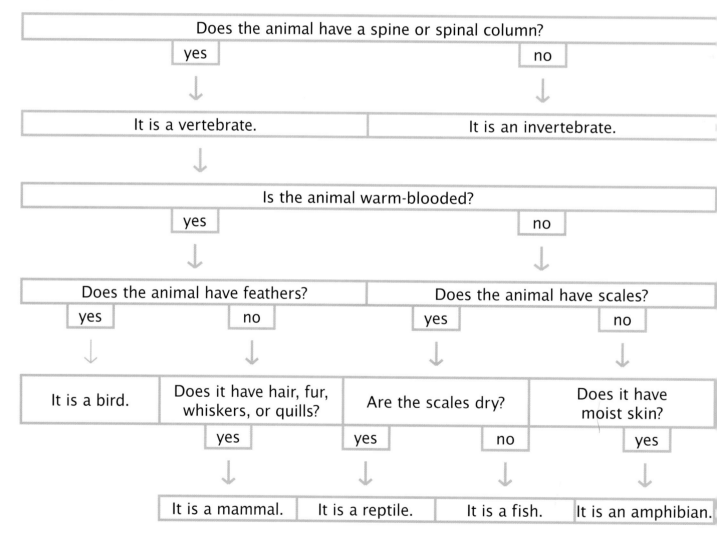

Mammal or Not?

Use the dichotomous key on the previous page to identify whether these animals are mammals or not. If it is not a mammal, identify whether it is an invertebrate, fish, reptile, amphibian, or bird. Answers are below.

Penguins have spines and are warm-blooded. They are covered in feathers and spend most of their lives in the water.

Humans are warm-blooded and have spines. Their bodies are covered in hair, not feathers. Humans live all around the world.

Dogs have spines and fur on their bodies. They are warm-blooded. Many dogs live with humans as pets (domesticated).

Snakes are cold-blooded and have spines. They have dry scales covering their bodies. Some snakes are venomous.

Honeybees have no spine. They are insects and live in a group called a colony. Honeybees build and live in hives.

Stingrays have spines and are cold-blooded. They are covered in small, moist scales and use gills to breathe oxygen from the water.

Toads have bumpy, moist skin. They have spines and are cold-blooded. Their bodies change from tadpoles to frogs in a process called metamorphosis.

Elephants are warm-blooded and have hair. Elephants eat plants and live in groups called herds. They have spines.

Answers: Mammal: dogs, humans, elephants. Invertebrate: honeybees. Fish: stingrays. Reptile: snakes. Amphibian: toads. Bird: penguins.

Some Mammals Are Different

There are more than 5,400 species of mammals in the world. Most mammals give birth to live young. Only two mammals lay eggs: platypuses and echidnas. Most mammals walk on land or swim in water. Only one type of mammal can fly: bats.

The platypus is a mammal that lives in Australia and Tasmania. They have webbed feet and a bill like a duck's. They have thick hair and a sleek body like an otter's. Their tails are broad and flat like a beaver's. The males have venomous spikes on their back feet. Platypuses spend much of their time in the water and live in dirt burrows along the shore. Female platypuses lay eggs that hatch after only 10 days. The babies are smaller than a penny. They rely on their mothers for milk and care until they learn to swim at 3 to 4 months old.

The echidna is a mammal that lives in Australia and New Guinea. They use their 7 inch (18 cm) long tongue to scoop out and eat ants and termites. Echidnas have long claws and are fast diggers. When they are threatened by predators, echidnas dig straight down into the ground to get away. Female echidnas lay eggs that they carry in a pouch for 50 days. An infant echidna is called a puggle. The newly-hatched puggles live in a burrow and are cared for by their mother until they are 7 months old.

About one-fifth of all mammals are bats. Bats live all around the world. Although there are other mammals that can glide through the air (like flying squirrels), bats are the only mammals that can fly. Most bats eat fruit or insects. Just one little brown bat can eat 1,000 mosquitoes in a single hour of hunting! Some people build bat-houses to attract bats and keep insects away. Bats are active at night and sleep during the day (nocturnal). They hang upside down to sleep in caves, barns, or tree branches.

Mammals Near You

You are a mammal. All of the people you know are mammals. If you have a cat or a dog, you have a mammal for a pet. What other mammals live near you? Anywhere you live—in the city, the suburbs, or a rural area—there are wild animals around you. Look for signs of mammals and other animals. Keep a journal of what you find.

badger   bear   deer   fox   otter   porcupine   raccoon   squirrel

Look for **tracks** (footprints). It's easiest to spot animal tracks in sand, mud, snow, or soft soil. Animals need water, so check for tracks in the dirt near a stream, pond, or other body of water. Bring a ruler with you so you can measure the tracks. Draw the tracks in your journal. You can look up tracks in a field guide to identify the animal that made the tracks.

Look for evidence of **feeding**. Has something been chewing on bushes, about 3 to 5 feet (1-1.5m) off the ground? There might be deer around. Is there a round, shallow hole in the dirt about 4 inches (10 cm) across? There might be skunks in your area. Look for chewed mushrooms, broken twigs and trees with bark gnawed off. These are all signs of animals feeding in the area. Draw them in your journal, especially if you can see any clear teeth-marks. Small mammals gather food and hide it in a log or underneath tree roots. If you find a pile of fruit, seeds, or nuts, draw it in your journal or take a picture. Don't move or take the food pile. The animal that put it there will be hungry and come looking for it later on.

Look for **scat** (poop). All animals poop. The kind of poop you find can tell you what kind of animals are in your area, when they were there, and even what they eat. Rabbits leave small, round balls that are usually yellow-green. Fox scat looks like dog poop, but can have pieces of the fox's food in it, like fur, feathers, small bones, or seeds. Deer have shiny, smooth, pellet-shaped scat. If you find animal poop, measure it and draw it in your journal. Try not to touch the poop when you measure it and be sure to wash your hands afterward.

Look for signs of **habitation**. Animals need a place to live. Some birds build nests. Some mammals dig burrows and dens. Some animals make their homes in the attics or crawlspaces of buildings. Other animals build their own homes, like beaver lodges or bee hives. Look for holes in the ground, especially near the base of trees. These might be the entrance to animals' burrows or dens. Any naturally-made hole—like a hollow log, rotting stump, knot in a tree, cave, or crevice in the rocks—is a good place for animals to live. Look for other animal signs, like tracks or scat, in the area. If you can see inside the hole, look for bits of fur or feathers that might have fallen off the animal. There might also be nesting material, like leaves, grass, twigs, that the animal uses to make their home more comfortable. Draw the entrance to the animal's home and anything you can see inside. Don't put your hand into any holes or animal homes—you might disturb the animal inside.

Thanks to Tiffany Vanderwerf, Curator of Education, and Emily Simms, Education Intern, at the Buffalo Zoo for reviewing the accuracy of the information in this book.

Library of Congress Cataloging-in-Publication Data

Hall, Katharine, 1989- author.
  Mammals : a compare and contrast book / by Katharine Hall.
      pages cm. -- (A compare and contrast book)
  Audience: Ages 4-8.
  Includes bibliographical references.
  ISBN 978-1-62855-729-9 (english hardcover) -- ISBN 978-1-62855-736-7 (english pbk.) -- ISBN 978-1-62855-750-3 (english downloadable ebook) -- ISBN 978-1-62855-764-0 (english interactive dual-language ebook) -- ISBN 978-1-62855-743-5 (spanish pbk.) -- ISBN 978-1-62855-757-2 (spanish downloadable ebook) -- ISBN 978-1-62855-771-8 (spanish interactive dual-language ebook) 1. Mammals--Juvenile literature. I. Title. II. Series: Compare and contrast book.
  QL706.2.H35 2016
  599--dc23
                                    2015034843

Translated into Spanish: *Mamíferos*
Lexile® Level: 610
key phrases: animal classification, compare/contrast

Bibliography:
Macdonald, David W. The Princeton Encyclopedia of Mammals. Princeton, NJ: Princeton University Press, 2009. Print.
Mammals. San Diego Zoo. n.d. Web. 04 March 2015.
Reid, Fiona. Peterson Field Guide to Mammals of North America (Fourth Edition). Boston, MA: Houghton Mifflin Harcourt, 2006.
Stewart, Brent S. and Phillip J. Clapham. National Audubon Society Guide to Marine Mammals of the World. New York, NY: Knopf, 2002. Print.

Image	Photo Source
Horses	Ellen Geddes, Maplewood Farm
Dog	Terry Hall
Silverback Gorilla	Paul Brennan, public domain
Dolphin	Momopixs, Shutterstock
Whale Skeleton	Paolo Neo, public domain
Cat	Claudette Gallant, public domain
Cat Skeleton	McCarthy's PhotoWorks, Shutterstock
Dolphin	NASA, USFSW
Dolphin skeleton	Risteski Goce, Shutterstock
Elk	Ryan Hagerty, USFWS
Goat	X Posid, public domain
Sea Otters	Karney Lee, USFWS
Otter	Vera Kratochvil, public domain
Bear	Adam Van Spronsen, Shutterstock
Manatee	Keith Ramos, USFWS
Pigs	Michael Stirling, public domain
Horses	Ellen Geddes, Maplewood Farm
Sea Lions	K Whiteford, public domain
Sheep	X Posid, public domain
Baboons	Peter Griffin, public domain
Beluga Whales	Rainer Plendl, Shutterstock
Children	Terry Hall
Penguin	Dean Bertoncelj, Shutterstock
Dog	Terry Hall
Honeybee	Jani Ravas, public domain
Toad	Gary M. Stolz, USFWS
Human	Terry Hall
Snake	Bobbi Jones Jones, public domain
Stingray	Petr Kratochvil, public domain
Elephant	Marina Shemesh, public domain
Echidna	Allan Whittome, public domain
Platypus	Bildagentur Zoonar GmbH, Shutterstock
Bat	Andy King, USFWS

Manufactured in China, December 2015
This product conforms to CPSIA 2008
First Printing

Arbordale Publishing
Mt. Pleasant, SC 29464
www.ArbordalePublishing.com